D0685142

THE RANSOM (

TOWN OF SUMMIT

HAVE A NICE DAY!

It is about one hundred years ago in America. Bill and Sam are in the town of Summit, but they are not having a nice day. They don't have much money – what can they do? Then Sam has an idea – kidnap! They hear about a rich family, the Dorsets. They hear about their son, Johnny. They want to take Johnny and then ask the family for money.

'He's a lot of trouble,' a woman tells them – but Bill and Sam don't listen. They find the big Dorset house and they find Johnny. 'He's a nice little boy,' they think, and they take him away.

But Johnny is a lot of trouble. 'My name is Red Chief,' he says, and he likes to play games . . .

OXFORD BOOKWORMS LIBRARY

Classics

The Ransom of Red Chief

Starter (250 headwords)

O. HENRY

The Ransom
of Red Chief

Retold by
Paul Shipton

Illustrated by
Axel Rator

OXFORD UNIVERSITY PRESS

OXFORD
UNIVERSITY PRESS

Great Clarendon Street, Oxford OX2 6DP

Oxford University Press is a department of the University of Oxford.
It furthers the University's objective of excellence in research, scholarship,
and education by publishing worldwide in

Oxford New York

Auckland Cape Town Dar es Salaam Hong Kong Karachi
Kuala Lumpur Madrid Melbourne Mexico City Nairobi
New Delhi Shanghai Taipei Toronto

With offices in

Argentina Austria Brazil Chile Czech Republic France Greece
Guatemala Hungary Italy Japan Poland Portugal Singapore
South Korea Switzerland Thailand Turkey Ukraine Vietnam

OXFORD and OXFORD ENGLISH are registered trade marks of
Oxford University Press in the UK and in certain other countries

This simplified edition © Oxford University Press 2008

Database right Oxford University Press (maker)

First published in Oxford Bookworms 2000

2 4 6 8 10 9 7 5 3 1

No unauthorized photocopying

All rights reserved. No part of this publication may be reproduced,
stored in a retrieval system, or transmitted, in any form or by any means,
without the prior permission in writing of Oxford University Press,
or as expressly permitted by law, or under terms agreed with the appropriate
reprographics rights organization. Enquiries concerning reproduction
outside the scope of the above should be sent to the ELT Rights Department,
Oxford University Press, at the address above

You must not circulate this book in any other binding or cover
and you must impose this same condition on any acquirer

Any websites referred to in this publication are in the public domain and
their addresses are provided by Oxford University Press for information only.
Oxford University Press disclaims any responsibility for the content

ISBN: 978 0 19 423415 3

Printed in Hong Kong

Word count (main text): 890

For more information on the Oxford Bookworms Library, visit
www.oup.com/elt/bookworms

CONTENTS

THE RANSOM OF RED CHIEF

Mr Ebenezer Dorset:

We have your son. Do you want to see him again?

Then you must give us a ransom of $1,500.

Give us the money tonight. There are three big trees near the Summit River. Put your answer in the tallest tree.

Do not tell the police about this.

From

What names can we put?

I know...

Two desperate men

Look at this letter, Bill! It's money in the bank.

To Two Desperate Men:

Thank you for your letter.
My answer is no.
The ransom is
very high.

I have another idea for you.
You bring Johnny home
and you give me $ 200.
When Johnny is with me
at home, you can escape.

Ebenezer Dorset

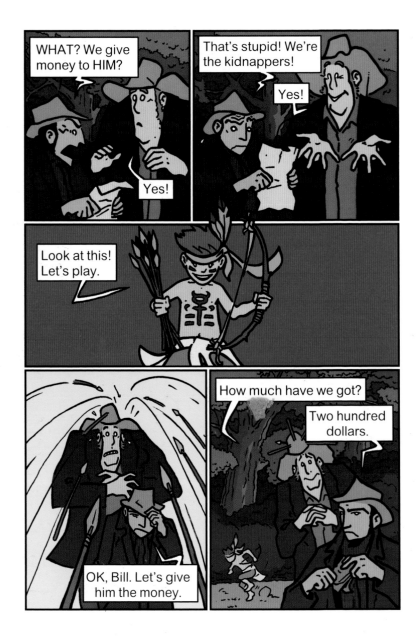

GLOSSARY

camping sleeping and cooking outside or in a tent

catch run after and take hold of

desperate *(adj)* having no hope

dinner a meal in the early evening

dream the thoughts or pictures you have when you sleep

fight *(n)* when two or more people try to win by punching or kicking each other, they are having a fight

heart the thing that pushes blood around the body

high *(adj)* expensive

hold *(vb)* keep something in the hand or hands

kidnap take somebody and only return them to their friends or family for money

knock hit with the hand

monster a very bad person

nose the part of the face above the mouth

ouch what you say when you are in pain

ransom the money that kidnappers ask for

rich *(adj)* having a lot of money

strong having a powerful body

trouble *(n)* a lot of problems, or something that makes a lot of problems

The Ransom of Red Chief

ACTIVITIES

ACTIVITIES

Before Reading

1 Look at the front and back cover of the book and guess the answers to these questions.

1 Who is Red Chief?

   a ☐ Sam.

   b ☐ Bill.

   c ☐ The boy on the front cover.

2 When does the story happen?

   a ☐ 100 years ago.

   b ☐ in the year 2000.

   c ☐ 500 years ago.

3 Imagine you are the boy on the front cover. How do you feel?

   a ☐ Happy.

   b ☐ Angry.

   c ☐ Afraid.

2 Read the story introduction on the first page of the book. How do Sam and Bill try to make a lot of money?

	YES	NO
a They take money from a shop.	☐	☐
b They kidnap a boy.	☐	☐
c They take horses and sell them.	☐	☐

ACTIVITIES

While Reading

1 Read pages 1–6.
Are these sentences true (T) or false (F)?

	T	F
1 Sam and Bill have no money.	☐	☐
2 They look for jobs in Summit.	☐	☐
3 Ebenezer Dorset is the richest man in town.	☐	☐
4 They decide to kidnap Ebenezer Dorset.	☐	☐
5 Johnny is afraid.	☐	☐
6 Bill stays with Johnny.	☐	☐
7 Johnny says he is called Red Chief now.	☐	☐

2 Read pages 7–12. Complete the sentences.

I'm .... Let's sleep.

It's a little ...., Bill. Do you want to hold it?

We must ....
a letter now.

Wait a ....!
Where's the boy?

3 Read pages 13–18, and match the following sentence halves to make five complete sentences.

1 Bill is afraid . . .
2 Johnny laughs . . .
3 Johnny runs away . . .
4 The old man takes the letter . . .
5 Johnny comes back . . .

a when Bill tries to catch him.
b when he can play games with Bill.
c when Sam goes to the shop in town.
d when Sam leaves.
e when Sam is back.

4 Read pages 19–24 and answer these questions.

1 Who brings Dorset's answer to the tree?
2 What does Dorset ask for in his letter?
3 What do Sam and Bill want to do?
4 How does Johnny feel when he sees his house?
5 How long can Mr Dorset hold his son?
6 What do Sam and Bill do when Dorset is holding Johnny?

ACTIVITIES

After Reading

1 Put these sentences in the correct order.

a ☐ Sam and Bill write a ransom letter.

b ☐ Mr Dorset does not pay the ransom.

c ☐ They run out of town.

d ☐ Sam and Bill take Johnny home.

e ☐ Johnny says that he is called Red Chief.

f ☐ Sam takes the letter to town.

g ☐ They kidnap Johnny Dorset.

i ☐ Sam and Bill arrive in Summit.

h ☐ They pay money to Mr Dorset.

2 Match the names and pictures with the words.

Sam   Bill   Johnny   Mr Dorset

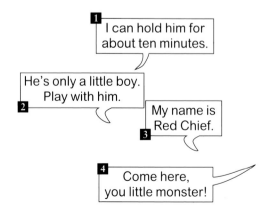

1 I can hold him for about ten minutes.

2 He's only a little boy. Play with him.

3 My name is Red Chief.

4 Come here, you little monster!

3 **Complete this summary of the story. Use these words:**
*afraid   arrive   boy   escape   fight   give   hits   money
name   spider   stays   ransom*

Sam and Bill only have $200 when they .... in the small
town of Summit. They want to kidnap the son of the richest
man in town. Johnny Dorset is a small .... but he gives Sam
and Bill a good .... They take him into the woods. Bill
.... with Johnny, while Sam takes the horses back to town.
Johnny says that his .... is Red Chief now. He plays and
plays with Bill! He puts a .... in his bed; he .... him on
the head. Soon Bill is very .... of the little boy!
Bill and Sam write a letter to Johnny's father. They ask for a
big .... But when Mr Dorset answers, he says no. He tells
Sam and Bill to give *him* .... Then they can .... from
Johnny! Sam and Bill say yes. They .... the money and then
run out of Summit.

4 **Write or draw a new ending for the story. Johnny escapes
from his father and runs after Sam and Bill. What happens
when he catches them?**

....
....
....
....
....
....
....
....

ABOUT THE AUTHOR

William Sydney Porter (O. Henry) was born in North Carolina, USA, in 1862. When he was twenty, he went to Texas where he worked in different offices and then in a bank. In 1887 he married a young woman called Athol Estes. He and Athol were very happy together, and at this time he began writing short stories. His most famous story is *The Gift of the Magi*, and many people think that Della in this story is based on his wife Athol. You can read this story in *New Yorkers – Short Stories* (Oxford Bookworms Stage 2); here it is called *The Christmas Presents*.

In 1896 Porter ran away to Honduras because people said he stole money from the bank when he was working there in 1894. A year later he came back to Texas to see Athol, who was dying, and in 1898 he was sent to prison. During his time there he published many short stories, using the name 'O. Henry', and when he left prison in 1901, he was already a famous writer. He then lived in New York until his death in 1910.

OXFORD BOOKWORMS LIBRARY

*Classics • Crime & Mystery • Factfiles • Fantasy & Horror
Human Interest • Playscripts • Thriller & Adventure
True Stories • World Stories*

The OXFORD BOOKWORMS LIBRARY provides enjoyable reading in English, with a wide range of classic and modern fiction, non-fiction, and plays. It includes original and adapted texts in seven carefully graded language stages, which take learners from beginner to advanced level. An overview is given on the next pages.

All Stage 1 titles are available as audio recordings, as well as over eighty other titles from Starter to Stage 6. All Starters and many titles at Stages 1 to 4 are specially recommended for younger learners. Every Bookworm is illustrated, and Starters and Factfiles have full-colour illustrations.

The OXFORD BOOKWORMS LIBRARY also offers extensive support. Each book contains an introduction to the story, notes about the author, a glossary, and activities. Additional resources include tests and worksheets, and answers for these and for the activities in the books. There is advice on running a class library, using audio recordings, and the many ways of using Oxford Bookworms in reading programmes. Resource materials are available on the website <www.oup.com/elt/bookworms>.

The *Oxford Bookworms Collection* is a series for advanced learners. It consists of volumes of short stories by well-known authors, both classic and modern. Texts are not abridged or adapted in any way, but carefully selected to be accessible to the advanced student.

You can find details and a full list of titles in the *Oxford Bookworms Library Catalogue* and *Oxford English Language Teaching Catalogues*, and on the website <www.oup.com/elt/bookworms>.

THE OXFORD BOOKWORMS LIBRARY
GRADING AND SAMPLE EXTRACTS

STARTER • 250 HEADWORDS
present simple – present continuous – imperative –
can/cannot, *must* – *going to* (future) – simple gerunds ...

Her phone is ringing – but where is it?

Sally gets out of bed and looks in her bag. No phone. She looks under the bed. No phone. Then she looks behind the door. There is her phone. Sally picks up her phone and answers it. *Sally's Phone*

STAGE 1 • 400 HEADWORDS
... past simple – coordination with *and*, *but*, *or* –
subordination with *before*, *after*, *when*, *because*, *so* ...

I knew him in Persia. He was a famous builder and I worked with him there. For a time I was his friend, but not for long. When he came to Paris, I came after him – I wanted to watch him. He was a very clever, very dangerous man. *The Phantom of the Opera*

STAGE 2 • 700 HEADWORDS
... present perfect – *will* (future) – *(don't) have to*, *must not*, *could* –
comparison of adjectives – simple *if* clauses – past continuous –
tag questions – *ask/tell* + infinitive ...

While I was writing these words in my diary, I decided what to do. I must try to escape. I shall try to get down the wall outside. The window is high above the ground, but I have to try. I shall take some of the gold with me – if I escape, perhaps it will be helpful later. *Dracula*

STAGE 3 • 1000 HEADWORDS

… should, may – present perfect continuous – *used to* – past perfect – causative – relative clauses – indirect statements …

Of course, it was most important that no one should see Colin, Mary, or Dickon entering the secret garden. So Colin gave orders to the gardeners that they must all keep away from that part of the garden in future. ***The Secret Garden***

STAGE 4 • 1400 HEADWORDS

… past perfect continuous – passive (simple forms) – *would* conditional clauses – indirect questions – relatives with *where/when* – gerunds after prepositions/phrases …

I was glad. Now Hyde could not show his face to the world again. If he did, every honest man in London would be proud to report him to the police. ***Dr Jekyll and Mr Hyde***

STAGE 5 • 1800 HEADWORDS

… future continuous – future perfect – passive (modals, continuous forms) – *would have* conditional clauses – modals + perfect infinitive …

If he had spoken Estella's name, I would have hit him. I was so angry with him, and so depressed about my future, that I could not eat the breakfast. Instead I went straight to the old house. ***Great Expectations***

STAGE 6 • 2500 HEADWORDS

… passive (infinitives, gerunds) – advanced modal meanings – clauses of concession, condition

When I stepped up to the piano, I was confident. It was as if I knew that the prodigy side of me really did exist. And when I started to play, I was so caught up in how lovely I looked that I didn't worry how I would sound. ***The Joy Luck Club***

38

BOOKWORMS · CLASSICS · STARTER

A Connecticut Yankee in King Arthur's Court

MARK TWAIN

Retold by Alan Hines

Hank Morgan is a happy young man in Connecticut, USA in 1879 until one day someone runs into his office and shouts, 'Come quickly, Boss! Two men are fighting.' After this, something very strange happens to him, and his life changes forever.

BOOKWORMS · CRIME & MYSTERY · STARTER

Give us the Money

MAEVE CLARKE

'Every day is the same. Nothing exciting ever happens to me,' thinks Adam one boring Monday morning. But today is not the same. When he helps a beautiful young woman because some men want to take her bag, life gets exciting and very, very dangerous.

BOOKWORMS · CRIME & MYSTERY · STARTER

Police TV

TIM VICARY

'Every day someone steals money from people near the shops. We must stop this,' says Dan, a police officer. The police use TV cameras but it is not easy because there are so many suspects – who is the robber?

BOOKWORMS · THRILLER & ADVENTURE · STARTER

Taxi of Terror

PHILLIP BURROWS AND MARK FOSTER

'How does it work?' Jack asks when he opens his present – a mobile phone. Later that night, Jack is a prisoner in a taxi in the empty streets of the dark city. He now tries his mobile phone for the first time. Can it save his life?

BOOKWORMS · CLASSICS · STAGE 1

The Adventures of Tom Sawyer

MARK TWAIN

Retold by Nick Bullard

Tom Sawyer does not like school. He does not like work, and he never wants to get out of bed in the morning. But he likes swimming and fishing, and having adventures with his friends. And he has a lot of adventures. One night, he and his friend Huck Finn go to the graveyard to look for ghosts.

They don't see any ghosts that night. They see something worse than a ghost – much, much worse . . .

BOOKWORMS · THRILLER & ADVENTURE · STAGE 1

Goodbye, Mr Hollywood

JOHN ESCOTT

Nick Lortz is sitting outside a café in Whistler, a village in the Canadian mountains, when a stranger comes and sits next to him. She's young, pretty, and has a beautiful smile. Nick is happy to sit and talk with her.

But why does she call Nick 'Mr Hollywood'? Why does she give him a big kiss when she leaves? And who is the man at the next table – the man with short white hair?

Nick learns the answers to these questions three long days later – in a police station on Vancouver Island.